5 STEPS TO DRAWING
MONSTERS

by Amanda StJohn • illustrated by Patrick Girouard

Published by The Child's World®
1980 Lookout Drive • Mankato, MN 56003-1705
800-599-READ • www.childsworld.com

ACKNOWLEDGMENTS
The Child's World®: Mary Berendes, Publishing Director
The Design Lab: Design and production
Red Line Editorial: Editorial direction

ISBN: 978-1-60973-202-8
LCCN: 2011927711

Printed in the United States of America
Mankato, MN
July 2011
PA02088

TABLE OF CONTENTS

What Are Monsters? 4
Monsters around the World 6
Monsters and Writers 8
Drawing Tips 10

Vampire 12
Loch Ness Monster 14
Cyclops 16
Ogre 18
Frankenstein's Monster 20
Yeti 22
Godzilla 24
Werewolf 26

More Drawing 28
Glossary 30
Find Out More 31
Index 32

WHAT ARE MONSTERS?

Monsters are ugly, scary creatures that live in our **imaginations**. Monsters come in many forms. They can be taller than the tallest buildings. They can be smaller than a mouse. Some monsters have sharp teeth. Some have green skin. Some monsters are clever and sneaky. Others are easily tricked.

The word *monster* means "sign." In stories, when people see a monster, they think it is a sign something bad will happen. Many scream and run away.

Many people have heard of the famous monsters. These monsters are the superstars. They are in books, movies, and cartoons all around the world. Pictures of their faces decorate our clothes, lunch boxes, and notebooks.

MONSTERS AROUND THE WORLD

There are tales of monsters in all parts of the world. The cyclops is a giant with one eyeball. It lives near the Mediterranean Sea. Godzilla is a huge dragon-like monster from Japan. In movies, it attacks and destroys Tokyo.

People say yetis live in the Himalayan Mountains. A yeti is an ape-like creature that lives in thick forest areas. It is often mistaken as a tall human. In North America and Canada, a similar creature has been spotted. Some Native American **legends** call the creature Sasquatch. This means "hairy man." The creature is also called Bigfoot.

Scotland is home to the Loch Ness monster. It is also called "Nessie." *Loch Ness* means "Lake Ness." Nessie lives in this lake. People claim to have seen Nessie with their own eyes. But no photograph is clear enough to **prove** she exists.

MONSTERS AND WRITERS

Writers have enjoyed creating monsters for their stories for a long time. Polyphemus is the cyclops in an old story called *The Odyssey*. Polyphemus ate four soldiers. Other soldiers blinded Polyphemus. Then they escaped.

In *Frankenstein,* a mad scientist named Dr. Frankenstein creates a monster out of parts from dead bodies. Dr. Frankenstein puts bolts in the monster's neck. He gives the monster a

shock of electricity. This brings the monster to life. Dr. Frankenstein is so afraid to look at his monster that he runs away. This makes the monster sad and very angry. Some people call the monster "Frankenstein" after his maker. But the monster does not really have a name.

People liked reading books about monsters. More writers created other monster stories, too. Today, people write about monsters in **horror** stories.

DRAWING TIPS

You've learned about monsters. You're almost ready to draw them. But first, here are a few drawing tips:

Every artist needs tools. To learn how to draw monsters, you will need:

- Some paper
- A pencil
- An eraser
- Markers, crayons, colored pencils, or watercolors (optional)

Anyone can learn to draw. You might think only some people can draw. That's not true. Everyone can learn to draw. It takes practice, though. The more you draw, the better you will be. With practice, you will become a true artist!

Everyone makes mistakes. This is okay! Mistakes help you learn. They help you know what not to do next time. Mistakes can even make your drawing more special. It's all right if you draw a monster's eyes too big. Now you've got a one-of-a-kind drawing. You can erase a mistake you don't like, too. Then start again!

Stay loose. Relax your body before you begin. Hold your pencil lightly. Don't rest your wrist on the table. Instead, move your whole arm as you draw. This will help you make smooth lines. Press lightly on the paper when you draw or erase.

Drawing is fun! The most important thing about drawing is to have fun. Be creative. Your drawings don't have to look exactly like the pictures in this book. Try changing the shape of the monster's head or how many eyes it has. You can also use markers, crayons, colored pencils, or watercolors to bring your monsters to life.

1

2

VAMPIRE

3

4

Vampires drink blood to stay alive. Often, blood drips from their fangs. Vampires wear long capes. When they turn into bats, the capes turn into wings.

1

2

LOCH NESS MONSTER

3

4

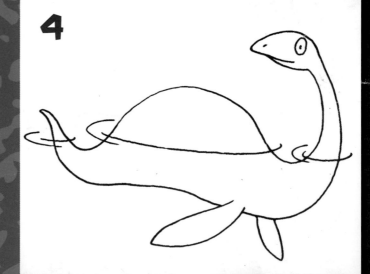

The Loch Ness monster has a small head and a large body. Some people believe it might be a relative to a type of dinosaur that lived in water.

1

2

CYCLOPS

3

4

A cyclops may live in a cave. Or it might live in a volcano where it is very hot. This makes it sweaty, smelly, and crabby.

1

2

OGRE

3

4

18

Most ogres have over-sized heads and big muscles. They are not smart or polite. They drool and burp a lot. Ogres move slowly. They trip easily, too.

5

1

2

FRANKENSTEIN'S MONSTER

3

4

Frankenstein's monster is made from body parts that are sewn together. The monster may have ended up with too many bones. This makes it taller than humans.

1

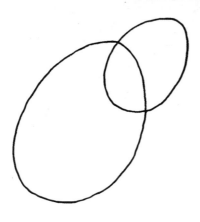

2

YETI

3

4

Some people believe a yeti can weigh up to 900 pounds (408 kg). It can be 11 feet (3.4 m) tall. It has a cone-shaped head and long, shaggy body hair.

1

2

GODZILLA

3

4

Godzilla is a mixture of *Tyrannosaurus rex* and *Stegosaurus*. It has been in many Japanese movies. Godzilla breathes fire.

1

2

WEREWOLF

3

4

Werewolf means "wolf man." Normally, a werewolf looks like a man. But a werewolf changes into a hairy, toothy wolf during a full moon.

5

MORE DRAWING

Now you know how to draw monsters. Here are some ways to keep drawing them.

Monsters come in all different colors, shapes, sizes, and textures. You can draw them all! Try using pens or colored pencils to draw and color in details. Experiment with crayons and markers to give your drawings different colors and textures. You can also paint your drawings. Watercolors are easy to use. If you make a mistake, you can wipe it away with a damp cloth. Try tracing the outline of your drawing with a crayon or a marker. Then paint over it with watercolor. What happens?

Drawing Using Your Imagination

When you want something new to draw, all you have to do is use your imagination! What kinds of monsters can you dream up? Before you start, think about your monster. Is it big or small? What color is it? Does it have sharp teeth or a tail? Does it have fur, scales, stripes, or spots? Where does your monster live? Now try drawing it! If you need help, use the examples in this book to guide you.

GLOSSARY

horror (HOR-ur): If something is horror, it is meant to cause fear. Horror stories have scary monsters in them.

imaginations (ih-maj-uh-NAY-shuns): Imaginations are the abilities of people's minds to form pictures of things that are not present or real. Monsters are created in imaginations.

legends (LEJ-unds): Legends are stories that have been handed down over many years. Some legends have monsters in them.

prove (PROOV): To prove means to show that something is true. People have not been able to prove the Loch Ness monster exists.

FIND OUT MORE

BOOKS

Barr, Steve. *1-2-3 Draw Cartoon Monsters*. Columbus, NC: Peel Productions, 2004.

Lichtenheld, Tom. *Everything I Know About Monsters*. New York: Simon & Schuster, 2002.

Stephens, Jay. *Monsters! Draw Your Own Mutants, Freaks, & Creeps*. New York: Lark Books, 2007.

WEB SITES

Visit our Web site for links about drawing monsters:

childsworld.com/links

Note to Parents, Teachers, and Librarians: We routinely verify our Web links to make sure they are safe and active sites. So encourage your readers to check them out!

INDEX

cyclops, 6, 8, 17

drawing tips, 10–11, 28–29

Frankenstein's monster, 8–9, 21

Godzilla, 6, 25

imagination, 4, 29

Loch Ness monster, 7, 15

ogre, 19

size, 4, 6, 15, 19, 21, 23

stories, 5, 6, 7, 8, 9

vampire, 13

werewolf, 27

yeti, 6–7, 23

ABOUT THE AUTHOR:
Amanda StJohn is a poet and children's book author from Toledo, Ohio. Whenever possible, she and her mother watch classic monster movies together.

ABOUT THE ILLUSTRATOR:
Patrick Girouard lives and works in Indiana with his sweetheart, Debra, and their dog, Max. Patrick made his drawings on paper with ink and then painted them digitally.